TRUTH and SYMBOL

TRUTH and SYMBOL

from

VON DER WAHRHEIT

by

KARL JASPERS

Translated with an Introduction

by

Jean T. Wilde, William Kluback and William Kimmel

TWAYNE PUBLISHERS § NEW YORK

Truth and Symbol is taken from
Von der Wahrheit, originally published by
R. Piper & Co. Verlag, München, Germany, © 1947

MANUFACTURED IN THE UNITED STATES OF AMERICA BY
UNITED PRINTING SERVICES, INC.
NEW HAVEN, CONN.

TRUTH and SYMBOL

Introduction

Since Descartes, the subject-object dichotomy in consciousness has been one of the central problems (perhaps *the* central problem) of philosophy. Karl Jaspers' interpretation of this problem arises from the failure of German Idealism, both Subjective and Objective, to overcome the dichotomy which arises from Kant's distinction between the reflective and determinant judgments.

The undermining of the rational, cosmological solutions of Hegel and Schelling and the attack upon positivism by Kierkegaard and Nietzsche prepared the way for the emergence of a new interpretation of the subject-object dichotomy. This was already explored by the later Schelling in his Munich and Berlin lectures. Schelling's "positive" philosophy, in contrast to his earlier Objective Idealism, emphasized the existential rather than the essential (rational) character of the subject in thought. He disclosed the impossibility of overcoming the historical and unique concreteness of the existing subject in a movement of thought which makes of the subject a mere moment in the dialectic of reason. Accepting this position of Schelling, Jaspers further denies the positivist claim that the subject can be fully explained by analytical reason. The full dimensions of the subject cannot be exhausted by a rational examination of its own structure.

Kierkegaard and Nietzsche, though from different

points of view, had emphasized the non-rational dimension of existence which is both below and beyond the grasp of reason. For them this non-rational dimension is the source out of which the existing self emerges to become conscious of itself as subject, and also that which it encounters at the limits of empirical existence as the possibility of transcendence toward authentic selfhood. This movement of transcendence was accomplished by Kierkegaard in the "leap" of faith and by Nietzsche in identification with the Will to Power.

The attack of Schelling upon Hegel and the Kierkegaard-Nietzsche attack upon positivism provide the background for Jaspers' thought. For him the fundamental question is to discover how philosophy can disclose the transcendent ground of empirical existence and so provide a path toward authentic selfhood. Both Nietzsche and Kierkegaard had attempted to overcome the subject-object dichotomy on the basis of subjectivity and transcendence alone and so lost the concrete and empirical world.

Jaspers' analysis of the function of the cypher in philosophical thought, which is here presented in translation, constitutes the final section of his monumental work, *Von der Wahrheit*.[1] He begins this analysis with

---

1. It is neither possible nor desirable in this introduction to analyze the foundations of Jaspers' metaphysics. Some clarification of key concepts, however, is indispensible for the reading of this text.

In his *Reason and Existenz* he develops his method of dealing with the problem of reason and Being. The oldest problem for philosophy, and the one which is always and continually new, is the search for Being, for that which is the essential reality of the self and its world. It is the search for that toward which

an examination of the limits of all attempts to resolve the subject-object dichotomy on the basis of either the subject or the object alone. The limitation of such attempts brings him to his exposition of the function of cypher and symbol in illuminating the subject-object polarity.

The empirical world is not self-explanatory. At the limits [*Grenzen*] of all knowledge and all objects of knowledge and of the knowing self as the subject of

---

thought, in its never ending reflection upon the nature of the self and the world, continually moves but which it never adequately grasps. It always disappears just beyond the determinate forms of our knowledge, encompassing it while not being fully encompassed by it. As the source, basis, and condition for all particular beings and modes of being, for both the objects of reflection and for reflection itself, it is never exhausted by them and, therefore, never becomes an object for knowledge. As the foundation of all that thought encompasses and can encompass, it yet encompasses both thought and its objects, thinker and his world, as the all-encompassing and all-comprehensive. "The Encompassing [*das Umgreifende*] appears and disappears for us in two opposed perspectives: either as Being itself, in and through which we are—or else as the Encompassing which we ourselves are, and in which every mode of Being appears to us." It is the ultimate, self-supporting ground of Being, whether Being in itself or Being as it is for us.

The Encompassing that I am appears first not as the Encompassing itself but in three modes:

1. as an empirical existent,—an actual, living feeling, and perceiving body and soul united with empirical existence—the all-embracing, incomprehensible "other" which is Nature. I am a being among beings.

2. as consciousness as such in which Being appears to me in those timeless forms in which thought communicates its world. I am a conscious subject with objects for thought.

3. as spirit—the totality of intelligible thought, action, and feeling through which the world of experience is clarified and comprehended as meaningful, whole, and purposeful under the

knowledge, the self becomes aware of its finiteness and the finitude of reason.[2] Death, suffering, conflict, and guilt, on the one hand, and error, ambiguity, unsolvable antinomies, and the meaninglessness of absolute relativities, on the other, are symptoms of the limits of finitude on which the self and reason founder [*scheitern*].

This foundering of reason, however, is not necessarily final but may be the occasion for the discovery that reason does not exhaust the possibilities of understanding the self and its world and that there are possibilities that transcend the limits of empirical knowledge. The limit situation may then be recognized not only in its

---

form of Ideas, in the realm of philosophy, art, revelation, and history.

But in all its questioning about Being through these modes of Encompassing, consciousness never succeeds in grasping Being itself which always disappears just beyond it and its modes as that which transcends them by being their source and condition and ultimate horizon. This last frontier which contains within itself all the boundaries of all modes of Encompassing and which itself has no boundary is the Encompassing itself, Being itself, which, therefore, cannot be encompassed or circumscribed, but which can appear as Transcendence for Existenz.

This last pair of terms points to the ultimate confrontation of the Encompassing that we are, Existenz, with the absolute Other of reason and of Existenz, the always hidden and nameless Transcendence. In the encounter with Transcendence I discover the fundamental origin and condition of my selfhood. I discover myself to be "given to myself" as possibility, obligation, and task. I discover that my being is *my* being in the unconditioned freedom, possibility, and claim of the unrepeatable, historical moment. I discover my authentic selfhood—my Existenz.

2. We distinguish here between two uses of "reason." As used above, "reason" signifies the discursive, ratiocinative activity of thought. On the other hand, for Jaspers "reason" functions as that which binds together all the various modes of Encompassing.

negative form as the limitation upon which the mind founders and beyond which it cannot proceed, but also in the positive form of boundary or horizon which opens into new possibilities and dimensions for the self and for reason. The finite world no longer appears closed upon itself but at all its boundaries opens into Transcendence. In the encounter with Transcendence reason fulfills itself. In the encounter with Transcendence I discover authentic selfhood—my Existenz. In the encounter with Transcendence the being of the world appears authentically and ultimately real.

Empirical experience [*Realität*] represented by the subject-object dichotomy hovers in a state of suspension [*schwebt*] between two possibilities. When this structure is conceived to be self-sufficient in its finitude and attempts totally to account for itself in terms of itself, there follows inevitably and ultimately one or another form of foundering—skepticism or the despair of the possibility of knowing, ethical impotence, loss of meaning and value, multiple forms of demonic distortion, such as superstition, tyranny, and anarchy, and various forms of nihilism. When, on the other hand, in our encounter with the world of phenomena, we are able to encounter the transcendent ground of all its modes of being, we become conscious of the fact that the limits of the phenomenal world are surpassable, that the objects of empirical experience are not the ultimate ends of knowledge but are the bearers of meaning that transcend their empirical dimensions, and that the self is grounded in that which transcends its finite limits.

In such an encounter the object in its mere objectness

11

disappears and assumes the state of cypher [*Chiffer*]. The object-as-cypher cannot become an object of universal knowledge, available at all times for manipulation and analysis. As a cypher of Being it appears only in the unique encounter of an historical self with the sensuously concrete.

However, the essential reality [*Wirklichkeit*] of the world of phenomena appears not in its sensuousness as such, but in its transparency, its openness to the Other which encompasses it at all its boundaries and which this very sensuousness makes present. To adhere absolutely to the sensuous brings about a loss of the transparency of its cypher-status, the opaque and veiled character of empirical reality, and the ultimate foundering of reason. On the other hand, the rejection of the sensuously concrete in exclusive adherence to Transcendence leads to still other forms of foundering. In either case the result is a destruction of the subject-object polarity and a consequent loss of the consciousness of Being. The subject-object dichotomy is overcome only in an encounter with the world as cypher. The world of phenomena becomes the cypher-script of Being. The world-as-cypher is the mediation between the Being that I am (my Existenz) and the absolute Objectivity of the Being that is Being or Other for me (Transcendence).

The encounter with the cypher of Being is always unique, that is, the encounter of a particular existing self with the sensuously concrete at a specific time. It is, therefore, concrete, individual, and historical.

There is no direct communication of the encounter with the cypher of Being. It is communicated through the

various forms of religious, philosophical, and artistic expression, that is, through the cypher-script of man. Religious and artistic symbols and images and philosophical categories are concretizations of the cypher-script of
Being embodied in the forms of human thought and expression which themselves become occasions for further
encounter with Transcendence. This is possible, however, only when such forms of human thought and expression are not considered to be *merely* forms of human
thought and expression but are recognized to be cyphers
which lead back to the original encounter in which they
have their source. They are always threatened, however,
by the possibility of slipping from their cypher-status into
the status of objects among the other objects of the
empirical world. Then they become distorted or empty
forms of thought—"special" objects or copies of objects,
signs or allegories, self-sufficient objects of aesthetic
pleasure, intellectual concepts, or mental operations.

Jaspers describes this situation in the realm of philosophy. The ancient formula, "all philosophy begins in
wonder," defines the cypher character of philosophical
thought. The history of philosophy is for Jaspers a con-
tinuous reading of the cypher-script of Being through
the cypher-script of its own characteristic medium. When
his categories cease to be recognized as cyphers and become, for the philosopher, mere tools or mental operations, he ceases to philosophize. When, on the other
hand, the philosopher claims ultimate and final validity
for his thinking, he falls into the tyranny of dogmatic
metaphysics.

In reflective thinking the philosopher does not merely

pursue the course of his thoughts as though they were themselves determining the structure of the real. Genuine philosophy is a thinking which is also a "listening." It is the philosopher's "listening" to that which his thoughts, as mere forms of communication, veil or conceal, but which can speak out of these forms at their boundaries where they cease to be mere thoughts and are "heard" as the cypher-script of Being. Genuine philosophizing consists in watching for that which disappears just beyond thought and thinking. It is watching for what thought conceals just at the boundaries of what it discloses. Genuine philosophizing is the hovering [*Schweben*] of thought at the frontier between itself and the Other which thought makes present but which transcends thought at its boundary. The Self [Existenz] and Transcendence confront each other through the mediation of thought-as-cypher.

Philosophy is a reading of the cypher-script of Being through the cypher-script of its own categories. But this cypher reading is only possible through the involvement of the philosopher in his thought. The question then arises about the limitations that spring from the philosopher's historicity. Jaspers, following Dilthey's concept of the world-view, has shown in his *Psychologie der Weltanschauungen* the relative point of view of every interpretation of an encounter with Being. Historical consciousness recognizes that no philosophical system can exhaust the totality of Being; each is limited and conditioned by a world-view. No world-view can overcome its own historical position. The claim of any world-view to represent a universal perspective transcending its own historical position leads to a foundering of reason in demonic distortion. Nevertheless, within the limits and conditions of each world-view, Being itself is encountered. That which transcends the historical situation of the philosopher can, and in all great philosophers does, break through into his thought insofar as he recognizes its cypher-character.

Philosophizing demands the continual re-reading and re-hearing of past philosophizing. The re-reading of past philosophy is not simply a re-enacting of the thought processes of another age and an identification for a moment with its world-view. Nor is the reading of past philosophy a scavenger hunt for that which is still valid for thought in the ruins of that which time has rendered useless, as though one could thereby gradually build up a body of essential truths that would withstand change. When past philosophy is read as the cypher-script of Being, one is led, as the philosopher is, to an encounter with Being itself at its source. Listening to his thoughts as I follow them I find myself face to face not with a philosopher and his ideas but with the Transcendence that spoke to him through them. Historical thinking is not an encounter with the past but with Being itself through the cypher-script of the past. In this way Jaspers overcomes the limitations of the absolute relativity of historical world-views. He also proceeds further to overcome the limitations of philosophizing from within a given tradition. In one sense, the history of cypher-reading in thought is cumulative, that is, reality becomes more and more rich and varied in the multiplication of its forms. In this respect revelation is progressive. But it is not at all progressive in the sense of a gradual encompassing of more and more reality until, at some distant time, thought will have totally encompassed Being.

In his last work, *Die grossen Philosophen,* Jaspers undertakes a world history of philosophy. Socrates, Buddha, Confucius, Jesus, Plato, Augustine, Kant, Anaximander, Heraclitus, Parmenides, Plotinus, Anselm, Spinoza, Laotze, and Nagarjuna are the subjects of the first volume. One of man's supreme achievements is that genuine communication from person to person when, from out their historical situation in their search for the ultimate meaning of existence, the Transcendent breaks into thought, revealing to each the authenticity of his Selfhood and their common ground in the Encompassing. The history of philosophy is such a never-ending dialogue of person with person from out the depths of their historical situation and tradition through the cypher-script of thought and its encounter with Being itself, a dialogue in which all great men have participated and continually do participate. The ultimate aim of history and of philosophy is the unity of mankind. This unity can be gained only "from the depth of historicity, not as a common, knowable content but in boundless communication of the historically different in never-ending dialogue." The unity of mankind is essentially neither geographic nor historically cumulative but can result from a communication which transcends the cultural limitations of man and speaks both of man's encounter with Being and of man addressed by Being. The human community arises from participation in the communication of Being, insofar as the Being encountered in philosophical experience transcends all world-views and traditions. The history of philosophy for Jaspers is the conversation through the ages about Being in which each philosopher participates insofar as he is encountered by Being.

Cloaked in an historical garb, man has read the cypher-script of Being from which emerges the consciousness that each encounter with Being is the realization of a communicative path encompassing mankind. The structuring of this path is determined by the specific historical situation in which Transcendence is encountered through the cypher-possibility of empirical reality. In the encounter with Transcendence man discovers not only that he transcends the historical situation vertically in that he discovers that his authentic self is grounded in Being itself (his Existenz) and that he is addressed from outside the historical situation by Being itself (Transcendence), but also horizontally in that his historical situation is open toward the future for the actualization and communication of new forms in which Being can be communicated. Herein lies his freedom, that while he is bound to his historical situation it is this very situation which makes possible both his own and its transcendence.

In the consciousness of his authentic selfhood he becomes aware not only of his freedom as this possibility but also as his responsibility and obligation. In his encounter with Transcendence it is not the abstraction man that is addressed but he himself as this unique and irreplaceable Self in this specific situation, and therefore, the responsibility for the actualization of freedom is specifically his. In other words, Jaspers would say that man is obligated to be free.

In terms of the vertical dimension of the encounter, the Self is metaphysically free from all absolute claims of the empirical world. But in terms of the horizontal dimension of the encounter he is free only in responsible engagement in the concrete forms in which his empirical life is lived, not as ultimate realities but as cyphers of Being.

Objectivity as Cypher (Symbol)

Reason in its unending movement finds a foothold through an Objectivity [*Objektivität*][1] in which love has its fulfillment.[2] This Objectivity can no longer be any one of the objects [*Objekt*] which become objects [*Gegenstand*] of knowledge. For the completion of truth is not attained in an object as an end of knowledge, but in something objective, which transcends all empirical knowledge, something which is not really an object, in something objective which we call cypher or symbol or metaphor.

We should like to interpret cypher-status as constituting the completion of the consciousness of Being. For this, it is necessary first to realize once again that everything that is Being for us can be grasped only in the subject-object polarity. Being must assume a mode of being-an-object and at the same time a mode of subjectivity for which this is an object.

---

1. Jaspers' distinctions between *"Objekt," "Gegenstand"* and *"Objektsein,"* and between *"Objektivität"* and *"Gegenständlichkeit"* present difficulties in translation. Where he refers to the full and complete objectification of Being we have retained the capitalized form "Objectivity." *"Gegenständlichkeit,"* i.e., being a perceptible object, we have rendered "objectness." *"Objektsein,"* i.e. the state of being an object, we have rendered variably "object-status" or "being-an-object." Elsewhere, when the context is clear, we have used simply "object" and "objectivity." All footnotes are the translators'.

2. This analysis of the cypher follows directly after, and proceeds from Jaspers' treatment of love in *Von der Wahrheit*.

1

The Grasping of Being in the Subject-Object Polarity

It is necessary to recall the fundamental phenomenon which was clarified in the theory of knowledge: whenever we are and know consciousness, we are standing in the polar relationship of subject and object. Knowledge is a state of being directed towards an opposite other.

Knowledge first of all requires objectness [*Gegenständlichkeit*] (for without it no thought is, in fact, possible); secondly, perceptibility (for without it there is, in fact, no content, no stuff, no differentiation); thirdly, validity (for without it there is no certainty of conscious knowledge).

Objectivity, therefore, comprises these three at first separable moments: it signifies objectness (being-an-object), perceptibility (being-a-thing), validity (being-a-claim to affirmation or to perception).

In order that Being may be for us, it is necessary that in the polarity of subject and object, through perception, imagination and representation in experiencing [*Erleben*], and experience in general [*Erfahrung*], Being become present. And therefore, whenever we feel, surmise or sense, even ever so dimly, there is in us an urge towards clarity, that is, an urge to grasp perceptibly and validly in an objective form this presentness[3] which is dim, lacking the pregnancy of the subject-object polarity through which we first really become aware of it.

It is in accordance with this that we desire to possess not only every particularity of Being in its mode of being but also Being itself, the absolute, the all-causing, the unqualified, in the form of the objectness of an object, in the form of perception, through the validity of a correct proposition.

The grasping of Being does not, however, occur through a subject which would be an arbitrary point and which would have all Being solely in the opposite object. On the contrary, the being of the subject itself is the necessary condition for the presence of Being through a content which appears from out the depth of subjectivity. Consciousness of Being lies simultaneously in the grasping of the object and in the consummation of subjectivity.

At one time Being looks like an object in its fullness towards which an interchangeable subject-point (consciousness in general) is directed. Then, on the contrary, it looks like the content-full event of an ever single historical subjectivity which apparently merely attaches its own contents to the external point of being-an-object which obtains all of its content only through the movement of the subject.

On the one side stands the corporeality of the empirical world, the solidity of an observed and accepted

---

3. To preserve the distinction between "*Gegenwart*" and "*Gegenwärtigkeit*" we have used the terms "presence" and "presentness" respectively.

reality, the ontological objectivity of philosophically conceived Being. It seems as though the will to objectivity achieves the support of Being.

On the other side stands the present content of experiencing. I complete what Being is, when it is Being for me. It is not enough that the sun is shining. I must see it shine and that is more than a sense perception of the eye. It is an event of the entire subjectivity whose mood, ardor, and rapture feels the soul of a world radiant with sunlight.

In point of fact, however, there is no separated duality of subjectivity and objectivity. Both are inseparably bound together. The presence of Being is in the movement which grasps and permeates subject and object simultaneously. We take possession of Being in the polarity, but in such a way that subject and object mutually overlap. While we are directed towards the object, Being in its essence is not already before our eyes as an object but is present only in the Encompassing,[4] through object and subject simultaneously, as that which permeates both.

Each Encompassing in the polarity is not solely on one side as object or subject. The restriction to one side causes a loss of essentiality which does not, however, lie on the other side but in the modes in which object and subject are bound together in the polarity. Neither does

---

4. The "Encompassing" [*das Umgreifende*] is a key word in Jaspers' thought. It is not a word with a fixed, knowable connotation. It points to the all-inclusive comprehensiveness of Being itself as the foundation of all being and knowing but which itself cannot be grasped in concepts. Thus the Encompassing is at the same time the Comprehensive. Cf. Introduction, n. 1.

Existenz[5] lie in any way in the subject as such; Existenz appears in the interwining of subjectivity and objectivity.

The consciousness of Being has thus a double foundation in both objectivity and subjectivity. Always the animated soul in all the modes of its consciousness encounters the object as a being that is in itself, that is more than the soul and the thought which is being thought of, but which is not the act of thinking itself. The ultimate for the soul is always its subjectivity, the certainty that it is, the awareness of that which it is. The object can be raised to an absolute being-in-itself; subjectivity can no less be raised to the absolute. In the first instance Being is the substance, in the second, the ego. Both are false absolutizings of one pole. Each in itself leads to the consciousness of a groundlessness. Our consciousness of Being feels that Being is lost when it has nothing but the object, or is nothing but subject. Then in each case a reversal takes place in philosophizing. Whenever, in the objective knowledge of objects, the actual meaning of Being, and thereby essentiality and interest, cease, then the reality of Being is sought in a break-through to subjectivity (for example, Kierkegaard). Whenever, on the contrary, in the endless reflection of

---

5. *"Existenz"* and *"Transcendenz"* are also key terms for Jaspers and, like the "Encompassing" have no definable content. Existenz points not to man's existence in the world as this individual but as a possibility, an obligation, and a task of which he becomes conscious in self-awareness and in the presence of Transcendence. This latter word points to the frontiers of experience, the limit, or other, of reason, which Existenz encounters. Existenz and Transcendence represent the ground and the outer limit of being and knowing between which, and by virtue of which, the Encompassing of Being takes place.

subjectivity, in the merely speculative movement of thought, the object and with it the content has also disappeared, then the "break-through to the object" becomes a passionate desire of thinking (for example, the young Schelling). Each time appears the stern demand to return from groundlessness to Being. Such a polemic attitude usually leads from one extreme to the other.

A. *The polemic will towards the object.* When the sublime efforts of philosophic thought to achieve its purest expression arrive at self-misunderstanding in unfettered intellectuality, when reflection loses its ground and is arbitrarily dispersed into anything whatsoever, then thoughts revolve around themselves in endless circles, without content, in spite of every effort of the tormented head, no longer actually saying anything. Then the result is reversal. The violent urge towards grasping a ground is expressed. Thus the everyday realist in us insists upon reality, as against illusion, the moralist upon the absolute validity of law as against relativity, the aesthete upon form as against the nebulousness of endless movement, the ontologist upon the stability of conceptualized Being as against the dissolution of transitory being.

1. The everyday realist says accusingly that we are neglecting the world where it is empirically real and are indulging in dreams of what ought to be, in phantasies of ideals, or in abstractions. It is rather a question of the empirically real. This must be soberly recognized; it must be quietly obeyed. It is harsh and severe. We must not try to run away from it. Experience proves it.

The incontestable truth of this realism becomes invalid

when empirical reality is presumed to be wholly and conclusively known and when it claims to determine alone and absolutely what is at issue. Against this it must be maintained that the real world by no means is so simply present. Especially the human world is not adequately recognizable empirically as an existence which is, and always will be, just as it was perceived.

Rather the knowledge of reality is—as are from time to time its more unclear preliminary stages in the empirical assumptions of common practice—in each case a perspective into man's capability of objectifying. Such knowledge is correct and incorrect, is verifiable and unstable, and, as a credent knowing, is itself a reality, although it is one which can become radically different.

Thought works upon the reality of man. What thinking achieves in throwing light on impulses and in visions of possibilities, that is what transforms the thinking man. There is no absolute, permanent reality of man. Every action is like an experiment and the result shows, although again in no way unequivocally, whatever of reality was there, perhaps only in a preparedness which had not yet been realized.

What I think, is reality, if I do so not as a merely unconcerned play of intellectual possibilities of meaning which, in the process of thinking, I keep removed from myself, but if I think in such a way that what I have thought produces an effect in me.

To declare any reality of man as essential reality itself, signifies a neglect of the Encompassing. Kant rejects the "rabble of experience" at that point where the object of this experience is not a firmly established existent of

Nature but is man in his freedom and his possibilities. Here thought can bring forth and make what did not yet exist into an object of experience, that is, into reality.

2. The moralist insists upon the validity of laws, norms, and ideals and upon those, indeed, which are capable of being known unequivocally and which in each case indicate with inescapable definiteness what is correct and what is right.

The splendid truth of this position becomes invalid, however, when laws formulated in terms of a definite content are held to be always absolutely valid, at every time and in every situation. Then there steps into the place of the unconditionality of Existenz—which can also appear in an inflexible insistence upon obedience to law—an automatism which is emptied to the point of heedlessness.

3. An aesthetic position wills "form." It turns against the infinite relationships of things, against what is in the background, the nebulous, the fluctuating.

In it there is the urge towards objectivity in form, towards Being in a substance which can be possessed, towards the changeless over against the becoming.

In this there is truth as long as the cypher in the aesthetic objectivization of the picture is before our eyes and is read. It becomes untruth if the cypher is lost in favor of the free contemplation of forms. Then life becomes aesthetic contemplation, action becomes the enjoyment of feelings.

All Being is, as it were, congealed, even though in the most highly varied modes which allow for constant variation in its observation.

This Being, in momentarily fixed form, and separating into an infinite number of interchangeable forms, can be placed in the realm of the subjective as opposed to objective validity, or in that of the objective as opposed to subjective validity. It is necessary only that in each case there be a being, something unchangeable, which by observation and thought can be taken possession of in the image.

If this Being is placed in subjectivity, then the conscious aesthete is produced. He wants to experience and to hear continually the new, to experience it as interesting. But the decisive characteristic is that he wants to be and to remain as he is. He wants himself as being-thus, feels himself to be immutable, resists any possibility of change. He does not want inwardly to become himself. The "I just am like that" wards off every tendency to question. He can become ill, can be destroyed, but he can not become different. (It is a psychological question whether precisely those human beings who suffer under their hopeless mutability, their unreliable propensity to be different, tend towards such a position—human beings who express just that which they are not, but in such a form that the being-thus signifies an empirical actuality with which they ultimately affirm the unchangingness of their changeability.)

This is the direction of Schopenhauer's thought that man does not bring forth himself with horror or satisfaction in his life but rather through experience realizes what he unalterably is out of his intellectual ground.

In this aesthetic position everything transforms itself into ultimate validity in the form of perception and knowledge. If, for example, tragedy is brought into the framework of this attitude, then philosophical aesthetic knowledge, which claims to penetrate speculatively as though it were beyond that which has been thought, steps into the place of open tragic knowledge. This point of view tends to present systematically in tragedy misfortune of all kinds, which in itself should not be called tragic, or, failing to see the tragic in genuine tragedy, tends to recognize it erroneously. A sham salvation in contemplation permits the aesthetic attitude to accomplish emotionally and without consequences an uninvolved, unclear philosophizing. In the presence of the objectivity of the forms in the tragic, the aesthetic attitude can fall into pathos and enjoy its affects along with its own dispersedness and wretchedness, vanity and fearfulness in the world.

4. The ontologist tends to think of Being as itself, how it is in itself. He seeks satisfaction in knowledge of the essential, of its unfoldment, its distortions. He knows what Being is.

Thereby he approaches "sound common sense" which feels the need for a clear support for its thinking in the absolute object in itself and which, at the same time, wants the ease of the tangible which comes about through objectness and definiteness. The impulse towards the unquestionability of what has been thought seeks repose in something immediate which can be thought of reasonably and comfortably without further ado.

This ontological attitude is polemically opposed to every form of epistemological idealism, against those modes of thinking in a transcending manner in which the concreteness of being-an-object is lost in Being itself. It turns against all sublimated philosophies as against a robbing of essential reality, against abstraction and acrobatics in thinking. Whether it is in the tangibility of the sensuous object or of a thought reality, whether it is in the object of a cult or in the historically testified revelation, what is known is always satisfying simply by being there as itself. The ontological attitude clings to the drastic, rebelling against all other possibilities, and affirms the immovable.

Let us sum up. In the points of view described there is something common to all. What is otherwise highly heterogeneous coincides in one point, in being bound to the object as such. From this point of view, it creates a strange impression to let them all pass in review. They belong together:—

Everyday realism: philosophical ontology (especially when it surrenders the high philosophical achievement —because it has become acquainted with it in a contrived, somewhat neo-Kantian form—to a supposedly new object, Being, which is Being itself); Catholic Thomistic philosophy and the rationalistically conceived Objectivity of the dogmatic contents of faith; the aesthetic passion for historical form (while warding off the separating detours of genuine cognition); the just-wanting-to-be-like-that of the individual; the materialism of absolutized contents of knowledge (such as, of the "unconscious" of the psyche, or of biological facts, or of technical economic processes, in so far as they are regarded as Being itself), etc.

To be sure, they all combat one another, but on the

same level on which they belong to one another. They differ in what they consider to be Being but agree that Being is a tangible thing capable of being known, something that can be grasped in the object.

B. *The polemic will against the object.* In the enthusiasm of transcendental types of thinking in which everything which is only an object is melted down and evaporates so that Being is solely in the movement of thinking which projects the objects out of itself and takes them back—in this enthusiasm the object-status is not allowed to exist as such. It is considered to be reprehensible dogmatism to regard objects as having any being. It is stupidity to cling to and even to regard as real these lumps as though they were stones which could even be thrown at one's head. It is superstition to regard the object as having any being; indeed, the superstition is defined as the mental attitude which considers the self-subsisting object-status to be Being itself.

The truth of this contempt for the object lies in the resistance against being bound to the object, just as, on the contrary, the truth of the claim of the object is valid in its opposition to the disintegration of the object in subjectivity. For the truth of the contempt for the object is lost where the contact with essential reality is missing. The path of true philosophizing loses neither the subject nor the object in the appearance of Objectivity, but instead grasps Being in their polarity.

C. *Schematic antithetics.* In the opposition of the will toward the object and toward the subject it would be a mistake to decide in favor of one side. Polemically both are right in their opposition to the obliqueness of the opposing side, but are wrong in denying its peculiar kernel of truth. The conflict is resolved in the movement out of both sides in the Encompassing. The opposition and its alliance is to be expressed in variously modified categories. We sum it up once more in the contrasts of object and reflection, substance and function.

1. *Object and reflection.*

The one side: The object is itself. It is in direct relationship to seizing it immediately and essentially.

From there, reflection looks like a disturbance which withdraws from view the obvious and clear object-status, which abandons the ground together with observation and experience, and moves into the empty abstraction of a dizzy movement.

The other side: Reflection penetrates Being. It actually becomes aware of Being only indirectly, in the mirror and in the mirror of the mirror. For Being is fundamentally of the spirit, infinite in movement, dialectical.

From there, the mere object is an unpenetrated rigid thing, but falsely rigid. There is nothing positive in the immovable object-status, only a hindrance to revelation.

In truth philosophizing is an accomplishment in the encircling movement which overcomes this alternative. Genuine cognition holds what it has thought suspended between the already experienced and the new essential reality. Actual experience includes object and reflection in a totality. Both the dissolving reflection and the congealing objectivity of what is meant at any one time are annulled by being suspended within the movement of knowledge. The consummating frontier[6] beyond the limits of reflection and object is each time thinking in essential reality, thinking which has become essential reality.

2. *Substance and function.*

The one side: The passion for substance: it wants Being itself, the unshatterable, the eternally constant.

To this belongs the hostility towards the "functional" way of thinking, which annuls every substantial being and thereby Being itself. Functionalizing thinking dissipates; it destroys substance. The movement of thinking as such is to be overcome in the goal of repose in the presence of substance.

The other side: The passion for function: it seizes the entire world of objects as an appearance of Being in time, as the medium of the manifestness of the subject.

To this belongs the aversion to substance. This is a paralyzing dead-end. It is a false possession in time. It is that which is restricting, which destroys the ventures. It terminates seeking. It is the pillow on which rests the mind which is no longer knowing.

In truth philosophizing is accomplished only in the unity of substance and function in order to learn what is through the circular movement which expands and is fulfilled in infinity. Being itself is not substance; it is not in what is thought as something to be rounded off

---

6. Jaspers' term, *"Grenze,"* points to the limit of being and knowing and at the same time to the possibility of transcending the limit in the direction of Being itself.

as a work of thought, as something available as objective truth, as something existing in itself without me. Being is also not in function; it is not in the thinking of the subject as only a present reality of this accomplishment. On the contrary, Being is that which, through the reality of myself, I understand as that which is in itself, even without me, but which is possible for me to perceive only through my entire nature as the organ as it were, of the knowledge of Being.

D. *The problem of an encompassing Objectivity.* Since the Being of the subject-object polarity lies neither in the object nor in the subject, it is accessible only in both through the mediation of the one in the other. The mediation between object and subject is accomplished in all knowing. It occurs through movements from the one to the other, through operation of one upon the other, through dialectic changes of one into the other.

Now there is finally the comprehensive and yet special task of grasping Being in totality in the subject-object polarity through the mediation of both, and to do so in such a way that both are immediately in Objectivity. Nothing that appears in the subject-object polarity provides a ground which could be Being itself. We do, indeed, clarify the world in the polarity, allow definite objects to be comprehended, and carry out the acts of subjectivity in their particularity. But the development of this orientation of the world does not satisfy our consciousness of Being. This orientation is, to be sure, indispensable; it remains a constant problem and a matter of great interest. But it is not completed, and even the idea of its completion leaves us unsatisfied if it does not become the means of bringing us in touch with Being itself.

This task of actually taking hold of Being is fulfilled by the symbol (the metaphor or the cypher-status). That is now our theme. The cypher is neither object nor subject. It is objectivity which is permeated by subjectivity and in such a way that Being becomes present in the whole.

2

The Consciousness of Being
in the Cypher

In which sense Being can be present in the cypher (the symbol) must be discussed in greater detail.

A. *The path to the manifesting of the cypher.* The world and everything that occurs in it is a mystery. The crudeness of finding everything to be self-evident through force of habit and the mania for mystery to the point of the sensational and the superstitious must disappear where genuine astonishment begins. Philosophy illuminates the mystery and brings it completely into consciousness. It begins with astonishment and increases the astonishment. (Only false philosophy, which carries on its thinking like scientific research into the things of the world, casts out astonishment through an alleged knowledge.) Then the world as a whole and in every individual feature shows infinite depth. This mystery is quiet; in flaring up it becomes revealed in an unfoldment. And this mystery is essential; in it Being itself speaks.

All of our investigation grasps empirical reality. But in this investigation we can despair of encountering Being in its essence. In the process we reach just the point of noticing that we have passed by Being itself.

We become aware of the fact that in cognition we have moved in categories which, even in their totality, are like a fine filigree with which we grasp what at the same time we conceal with it. We bestir ourselves in order not to fall victim to any category. We should like to get through it and beyond it. Pushing ahead restlessly into the ocean of Being, we find ourselves always again and again at the beach of categorically secure, definite, particular knowledge. In contrast to the definiteness of the categories and of their restriction, in the symbol we become open to Being and at the same time filled with Being.

Our astonishment carries us rushing and plunging through the world into Transcendence. But we remain in the world and find ourselves again, not in Transcendence but in heightened presentness. Whatever there is for us, becomes more for us than it seemed at first to be. It becomes transparent, it becomes a symbol.

The symbol catches what would otherwise stream out of us and be lost in the void. The symbol shows what would, without it, remain completely hidden to us.

B. *The transformation of objects into the cypher.* The cypher is the object which is least of all only object, but rather in its being-an-object is already no longer an object like all other specific objects. As a cypher the object is, as it were, in suspension. In the very definiteness of what is objective, which is only its element, the cypher is lost. For it is itself not a definable object but that which encompasses both the subject and the object in what is objective. For this reason the cyphers are not still another new objective domain. They are not an objective conclusion. They are rather hidden in all objectivity. Everything that is, can be a cypher. It becomes a cypher through a transformation of the mode of being-an-object in the act of transcendence. While the formal transcending occurs through a movement of thought in which all objectivity disappears, this substantial transcending is a consummation of cypher-reading in which the concreteness, stability, and definiteness of what is objective vanishes at once in the suspended Objectivity which makes it possible.

Every mode of objectivity becomes a shackle if it is simply regarded as Being itself; the lack of objectivity, however, becomes emptiness also in subjectivity. Only in the polarity of subject and object is our life. In this polarity the object can attain that suspension which at the same time allows it to exist and elevates it. This suspension makes possible the consciousness of Being; for this the object is imbued from the depths with spirit. From this depth of Being the object obtains an irreplaceable meaning.

The object is not destroyed but is transformed in the mode of its being an object. This means that the object which is flat and opaque becomes transparent in the transcending. The object which is dull and speechless becomes the cypher (metaphor, symbol). The objectivity can be transformed because it contains hidden within itself Transcendence which shows itself in the transformation. Vice versa, if the power of things to communicate ceases, then they sink back into the lovelessness of indifferent uniformity.

C. *Character of the symbol.* The symbol is *com-*

munication [*Sprache*]. In the contact of the soul with Being it is the enkindling in which Being acquires communicative power. In this respect comprehension of the symbol is knowledge of Being; however, it is not a scientific knowledge of objects but a philosophical awareness of Being.

The symbol makes not only clear but *real* [*wirklich*][7] what would otherwise be like nothing. In the groundlessness of empirical realities [*Realitäten*] we gain a foothold, as it were, through symbols of essential reality. Being is not another reality which is hidden behind empirical realities. Within empirical existence itself the symbol speaks: in the concreteness of existing things we experience the essential reality of the symbol. There takes place a turning from the everyday thinking about concrete things toward an actual consciousness of essential reality.

The symbol is *infinite*. In pursuing the symbol, and with it the experience of essential reality, thought stands still. No thought is adequate to the symbol. The symbol opens us up for Being and shows us all Being.

But communication, essential reality, and infinity belong to the symbols only as long as they remain in the suspension of their appearance. As soon as they become definite images, fixed signs, and, thereby, things in the world, we again move with them to a beach, a beach of

---

7. Jaspers' distinction between *"Realität"* and *"Wirklichkeit"* can be rendered in English only by qualifying the word "reality." *"Realität"* refers to the empirically verifiable world of experience and has been rendered "empirical reality," "empirical existence" or "concrete reality." For *"Wirklichkeit"* we have used "essential reality" or "reality itself."

false corporealities, of mere images. The symbols, too, as transformed objectivities, must remain in the flow of intangibility. Their being-in-suspension alone constitutes their infinity. Their becoming-form makes it possible for them to collapse into fixed forms which are regarded as finite knowledge but henceforth provide no real support. Measured by empirical realities they are now only deceiving illusions.

The symbol is the complete presentness of Being. In it is the strongest, most penetrating mode of being present of whatever is. Essential reality is more, is inwardly more gripping, than the empirical reality which only dominates my daily life. If someone says, "God is more real than this table here," it is a distorted expression. In no way is God real like the table; it is a difference not of degree but of kind. Being bound by the absolutism of empirical existence closes one off from the essential reality of the Divinity. The assertion of God's existence as an existence greater than that of this table is a tyrannical form of the will to believe which, as a matter of fact, still clings to empirical reality as the absolute.

The cypher is listened to, not cognized. All talk about it, so unavoidable because the cypher only steps forth more clearly in communication, is already mistaken in its roots. For this reason the character of the cypher is only encircled but not reached if, in metaphor, we call it speech.

The characteristic of the cypher separates the signification from that which is signified in it. This separation is false. If we call cyphers a form of communication then the listening to the language *of the* cypher is itself a metaphor for something merely analogous but in itself quite different compared with our mode of listening to Being *in the* cyphers. The signification of the cyphers is not such that something present signifies something absent, a here signifies a beyond, but it lies simply in a presentness which is no longer translatable into knowledge of something. Being-a-cypher is a signification which signifies nothing else. Signification is itself only a metaphor for being-a-cypher. Language is a metaphor only when it is articulated by a cypher-status.

To call cypher-status a language is, to be sure, a metaphor corresponding to an object. We do, indeed, question the cypher as to its meaning. We attempt interpretations in regard to every cypher. With such clarification we experience at the same time a deepening of the cypher. But it becomes evident that no given interpretation suffices. The cypher is the inexhaustible signification with which no definite interpretation is commensurate, but which rather demands in the interpretation itself an endless movement of interpreting. Interpreting is not a form of cognition of the meaning of the cypher, but is itself a metaphorical act, a game. To interpret is impossible; Being itself, Transcendence, is present. It is nameless. If we speak of it, then we use an infinite number of names and cancel them all again. That which has significance is itself Being.

Finally, being-a-metaphor is itself only a metaphor, the transferring of a relationship in the world to this fundamental encompassing movement of Being in it.

The cypher is the metaphor which is Being, or the Being which is metaphor.

It is hopeless to make the categories apply, as definite categories, to the Encompassing. In such application the categories themselves change their meaning, become cyphers themselves, and so also the "reality" and the "infinity" which we attributed to the cypher.

What brings our consciousness of Being to fulfillment in truth cannot be made available as a content of knowledge. We circumscribe it in order to keep ourselves free for this truth, not in order to know what it is.

D. *The transparency of sensuousness.* Empirical reality has the characteristic of sensuous presence. Sensuousness shows at its borders the darkness of the unpenetrated, of the "being-thus." We lose Being when we veil the empirically real. We have to hit against the hardness of stark reality. Here is the inevitable outcome both for rational knowledge, which results in the mastery over things, as well as for contemplative observation which results in self-revelation by becoming transparent.

Philosophizing, in the transforming of the Being of objectivity into a cypher, creates free space for the movement toward Being itself. In it arises the unfettered, the infinitely possible. This, however, becomes real only in its being bound to what is sensuously present. It must for the moment speak effectively to this historical moment in such a way that eternity is in the now and Being is in the disappearing.

In order for Being to be in cypher-status, the sensuous present is, therefore, inevitable. The profoundest quality of Being must also appear and appear essentially in the sensuously concrete. In philosophizing, sensuousness is not abandoned but is endowed with meaning and soul.

For Being anywhere and at any time, the here and now of the sensuous present is, to be sure, the very least, the most indefinite condition. It shrivels together into the nothingness of that which is merely disappearing, which no longer persists. But in it all content is present which itself disappears and is no more if it does not assume the forms of a here and now.

Soil, landscape, and love, the institutions of communality, friends, the beloved, are for me not only the sensuous reality of perceptibility but the historical presence of Being itself.

Also the past is there for me only through the mode of its sensuous presentness. Only in this presentness does it show its content. The past is real for me only in so far as I experience it in its concreteness. This is then, as it were, doubly transparent as directed towards the past and through it towards eternal Being.

Transparency of sensuousness signifies at the same time disassociation from sensuousness as such. Absolute adherence to the sensuous draws one into the darkness of transparentlessness. The grasping of the content of Being in adherence to the sensuous goes beyond the sensuous.

There is no simple parallel between the fullness of the sensuous and the fullness of the content of Being. The consciousness of Being arises in the many layers of Being which crowd forth from the depth and whose immediacy and, as it were, mere surface is the sensuous present. The richest fullness of the sensuous can be poor in being without this depth. The most meager, perhaps only barely hinted at sensuousness can be a powerfully effective carrier of the depth of Being.

Since penetration into the depth of the sensuous present loosens the attachment to the sensuous as such, sensuousness becomes relative. Its empirical reality is no longer absolute Being. Consequently, man can find himself without foundation if the original, infinitely certain, nonsensuous content of Being, the essentially real within the empirical, is lost to him. The sensuous loses its value; the nonsensuous no longer remains. A sceptically experienced unreality surrounds man, neither essentially nor empirically compelling. He becomes abstract; he can no longer lay hold upon empirical reality since it has long since become veiled to him; he no longer believes in any essential reality since it has disappeared from him. In the dissolution of his consciousness of Being the impulses of his actions become capricious and arbitrary. (Since his existence remains, it is now unreasonably exposed to the forces of vitality, suggestion, blind obedience, and tyranny.)

To live in the transparency of empirical reality easily makes possible slipping into groundlessness. It seems that sensuous concreteness which, without transparence, wills nothing else than to be itself, is for most men a requisite for living. At any rate, the right truly to philosophize is only for people for whom the cypher, even in the meagerest of sensuous realities, is so unconditionally effective and is the real, just as sensuousness as such is for those who are sense bound.

For religions, in contrast to philosophy, the mode of

the sensuous presence of Transcendence is characteristic. In the cult, God is operative; in the saint, suprasensuous power. That God is tangible in the here and now—in the man Jesus—is a main thought of Christianity.

Augustine does not believe in the revelation of the Bible as a book of the past but he expressly believes only because the finite presence of the authority of the Church demands this belief.

This religious corporeality—if one compares it with being bound to transparentless realities—causes an upswing into the suprasensuous. Compared with philosophical presentness, however, it stands out from all other empirical realities as a distinctive empirical reality. It is itself a corporeal reality among other corporeal realities of the world. Not the transparency of sensuousness but the concreteness of Transcendence in a particular empirical reality of the world is, at any rate, the result. But what there might possibly be in the origin of true religion through such corporeality, or what the cult actually is, this is concealed from philosophy.

E. *The transparency of thought.* There are philosophical thoughts which, with a minimum of representation, bring about in the most extreme abstraction a full presence of the thinker: in thinking, despite the disappearance of the contents, Being is joined with Existenz precisely through this disappearance.

Thought itself becomes a cypher. No longer in the sensuous, but in thought, Being becomes present. It is the fascinating trait of philosophical speculation, how, unloosened from the sensuous, it confirms itself in the pure spiritualization [ideation] of Being.

To be sure, thought cannot be completed without a minimum of sensuous supports—signs, images, language —but this which is sensuously present is no longer as such that which is convincing but only that which is indispensable. It is the nobility of man to be able through the quiet contemplation of pure thought to transcend his entire sensuousness into this region of a spiritual self-affirmation.

This speculation is play. It is unreal. It leads as does thinking about objects, to a collapse of thought which, however, is precisely that which does the revealing. In the evaporation of all contents Being becomes palpable.

This never occurs, however, through thought alone. In thinking, something which is not this thought itself awakens, and something becomes apparent from the certainty of the existence of consciousness up to the source of Existenz in Transcendence. Rational thought as such, therefore, falls indifferently to the ground if that is missing which first gives it meaning and weight. It is the point at which I think without thinking about it, where I am myself present in thought. Real philosophy in the highest state of consciousness is yet unconscious in what is decisive. And yet it exerts itself unceasingly to render more conscious this that is unconscious. It is the restless movement which, in the steps of the thought which is becoming transparent, attains at times a moment of rest through that thinking which carries thought. In speculation there lies hidden what I cannot grasp in thought but which is given to us with thought through its movement.

3

The World of the Cyphers

Being is revealed through the symbol. The symbol is
suspended when I grasp essential reality in it. If it becomes fixed and definite and turns into an object in the
world, then it loses its essential reality. It collapses into
a sign, into a signification, into a metaphor. There are
such symbols in incalculable numbers which can be arranged according to multiple points of view. They con-
stitute the world of cyphers which, as an object of consideration, bears the same relation to its origin as does
the herbarium to living plants, or as does a collection of
bones to live bodies. As soon as we talk about the symbols,
we have completed this transformation. Only when in
thinking we proceed from the symbols in them [the cy-
phers], are we dealing with the essential reality which
speaks out of them. In detached talk about them, however, we prepare for the purer primary grasping of the
content of the symbol, just as when in handling bones or
straw we think of their origin. Then the encircling of the
symbols itself becomes a way of approaching it.

Two forms of thinking which at the same time veil
the essence of the symbols control such meditation about
them: 1) Symbols are, as the world of cyphers, a *special
domain of objects*, which is approached with questions

of order, source, transformation, and movement. 2) Symbols are *meanings* which are questioned as to their import, namely, as to what they mean.

A. *Source of the symbols.* A reading of the cyphers does not occur every time on the same level. It is not a matter-of-course procedure in which everyone simply accepts like every other person what the cypher says. It is rather with the upswing of man that the cyphers first become audible to him. They are not at all the simple thing which is at man's disposal at all times but they appear only in his transformation. They are that in which the whole man has a comprehensive understanding of what Being is. Therefore, cypher-reading is the primary requisite for authentic manhood. The cypher is always there, even though it may be primitive, flat, or distorted. Only he who recognizes the cyphers becomes man. At all times genuine reality for the essential man is in the cypher. But the cypher is also the final realization which at times comes forth for man out of his total and fundamental knowledge.

If we inquire about the source of the symbols, we obviously discover their original essence to be without source. It is not possible to get behind them. The question of their source is answered in a penetrating realization of their originality. What is to be investigated, however, is the forming of the symbols at their source.

The material of their appearance stems from the world of sensuous observations and of conceivabilities. But to lead the symbols back to this material is to misunderstand their essence and becomes a genetics which dissolves them.

The progress of their unfoldment can be observed in the intuitions of poets and artists and in the speculative thinking of philosophers. Their historical origin in the vision, in the rapture, in the revealing of essence [*Wesensschau*], in the transfiguration of reality on the part of great men—in Aeschylus, Sophocles, Dante, Shakespeare, Michelangelo, and Rembrandt, in Plato, Plotinus, Anselm, Cusanus, Spinoza, Kant, Schelling, and Hegel—can be demonstrated. Movements are seen passing from the sign to its unfoldment in the forms of art, from observing to thinking.

Thought is present in the symbol. The symbol is never without thought. It incites the thinking which, as in the discovery of the symbol, never reaches the end but always sees itself encompassed in the symbol. Thinking strives for the meaningful realization of the symbol's content. It falls into error through a finite determinateness of an interpretation of meaning. It teaches how to know the limits of a symbol and the necessity of changing the direction of listening. Thinking is led by rational logic from established definitions and tumbles into inescapable antinomies, or else it is led by the content of the primary symbolic experience and finds no end.

Whatever is attained from time to time in knowledge of the things in the world, not only destroys traditional symbols but makes new symbols possible. There took place simultaneously in Greece the development of philosophy and the elevating of mythical symbolism to its heights.

In connection with science and philosophy symbolism is progressively transformed from concreteness in superstition to the fluttering play among phenomena. To be sure, this brings with it at the same time the danger of the dissolution of the symbols into the state of unattachedness, but also the highest possibility of a free grasping of essential reality from out of the unconditionality of Existenz.

To discover symbolism as profoundly, as truly, as inclusively as possible, to adopt it from the poetic viewpoint and grasp it in its own thinking, is the concern of philosophy. Thought itself becomes a symbol.

The philosophizing man reads the cypher-script of Being by bringing forth a new cypher-script of thought. Being becomes present in form, in original image, in idea, and in all the modes of transcending thought-movement. To make the language of the symbols clear is the highest achievement of philosophical thinking.

The original philosophical thought is a cypher. This is splendidly visible in pre-Socratic philosophy but it was unconscious from the standpoint of method. It remains the basic trait of every great philosophy. At all times, however, there also takes place in philosophical thinking the defection from the cypher to the pure concept. Thinking which grasps the essential reality of Being turns into mere thinking; philosophy turns into presumptive science. Out of the manifold meanings of the cyphers grow the single meanings of concepts. Out of the infinity of the cypher, unfolding in the illimitable relations of thinking, grows the limitedness of definite thought.

In the philosophical cypher there is a mysterious interweaving of what is logically separated. Therefore, there is for mere understanding something unclarified and confusing in the philosophical cypher. All great philosophies seem to contain strange "errors," contradictions, and blurred borderlines, the disclosure of which, by making us aware of them, has the effect of causing the truth of the cypher to stand forth that much more purely. On the other hand, in merely fabricated philosophical thought-images, the showing up of these errors actually causes the dissolution of this attempt at thinking, which from the very outset is without content. There is, to be sure, no objective, rationally compelling criterion through which it would be possible to differentiate between the genuine unity of the cypher and the simultaneously logical and existential confusion of false philosophizing.

B. *Meaning of the symbols.* Thinking of the symbols through an "other" explains them genetically and dissolves them. Genuine symbols cannot be interpreted; what can be interpreted through an "other" ceases to be a symbol. On the other hand, the interpretation of symbols through their self-presentation penetrates into them but does not explain them. Such interpretation encircles and circumscribes, penetrates and illuminates. It becomes itself at once a part of the symbol. By interpreting, it participates in symbol-status. The symbol is not passed over by being understood, but is deepened and enhanced by being meditated upon.

The modes of interpretation are, therefore, to be tested as to their meaning, whether they destroy by explaining or whether they enhance by penetrating.

The explaining interpretation leads symbols back to confusions, transpositions, to error. While interpreting, it causes a freeing from the symbol and destroys it. This explanation points to the unconscious element of existence and dissolves in consciousness.

The penetrating interpretation, on the other hand, leads back to no "other." While interpreting it confirms the symbol; it liberates for the symbol. It points to the Transcendence of Being and expands the symbol.

Empirically verifiable interpretations are related either to meanings in the world, to the meaning of languages, of psychic expression, of the purposes desired by actions, of the meaning of man's intentions in what he has achieved, or also to phenomena of the body and the soul which inspire in connection with events, as though unconsciously something would be wanted, expressed, presented, or accomplished with them or through them.

Insofar as interpretations of the symbols are really verifiable, no genuine symbols are any longer in question, but rather either the first mentioned definite intraworldly relations of meaning, or illusions, dreams, or psycho-physical events. Interpretations which are genuine realizations have, on the contrary, no criterion of empirical verifiability but only the criteria of symbolic reality which is measured by itself.

The form of interpreting a meaning through an "other" sees itself before the symbols facing an infinite interpretability. This is appropriate as a movement of continual interpretation whenever this inappropriate form (interpreting by an "other") is used for rendering present the meaning of Being in the symbol. At the same time this movement through an orderly meaning-sequence in interpreting, with the cancellation of every particular

meaning of this total interpretation, can cancel up to
the consummation of the meaning of essential reality
rendered present in the symbol. This infinite interpretability, in the form of empirical interpreting in the direction of unconscious vitalistic events, becomes precisely
the distinguishing mark of the non-verifiability of such
interpretations in relation to empirical reality. Psycho-
analytical interpretations on the whole turn into a grimace
of cypher-script reading, as was suited to an era lacking
faith. Instead of pointing to the essential reality of transcendent Being, psychic unconscious events are pointed
to. Instead of illumination and faith, false explanation and
superstition are achieved.

If I interpret the soul of Nature, of the elements, of the
landscape, then I find no empirical meaning for expression (as in the expressions of the human soul), but
even more no absence of essential reality but rather the
presence of a being which appeals to us only in itself
and through itself. It is the same with all cyphers. They
do not permit interpretations in regard to an "other,"
but are the presentness of their content. I become aware
of them in a consciousness of their suspension in respect
to empirical reality. They speak through the very presence of an essential reality in their own language (where-
by "language" is used metaphorically only by analogy
with our language). Already in the "sign" as a symbol
essential reality is rudimentarily and inherently implicit.
In the unfolding of the symbol-content of the sign into
a work of art, the symbol does, to be sure, become rich
through consistent contemplation but in the fullness of
spirit it becomes empirically less effective. The sign com-

pels and puts everything upon me. The work of art is guidance through contemplation and by no means of its external form awakens and presents in definite, pregnant articulations what is lying in readiness within. On the outermost limits stand the elementary signs, from the primitive hieroglyphs of primitive man up to the sign posts at the frontiers and abysses of knowledge and of "God" simply as the name and sign which lacks all perceivable content.

The meaning of the symbols is that in them I encounter the essentially real. The fullness of reality is shown in them.

Whereas the idealist remains in himself in respect to all things and achieves the alleged absolute freedom to which, for example, Hegel's philosophy misleads him, but which at the end still leaves him actually without foundation, the man who understands symbols encounters essential reality in them. Their interpretation is reality itself. The question is how I experience it.

Reality always crystalizes itself in a definite manner as empirical realities in what is scientifically known. At this frontier it recedes into the ungraspable. It is arranged in levels of being, by being conceived, according to all categories, as contracting into the rigid bodies of a mechanism, into a substance, into an intellectual order, etc.

In contrast to this, reality itself is immediately present in the symbols. In them appearance and being are unseparated. Essential reality under the forms which it assumes in appearance, however, is not at all univocal. Rather there speaks to me out of it only what I can hear.

It is revealed to me according to my nature. Whatever I experience as fate and what and how I am able to love, that permits me to see reality. But it is not I who am the origin of mere representations in symbols, but rather reality is the source for what I experience in symbols. I am not able to hear reality in its totality and in its ultimate depth. It is more than I see and experience, but I experience it in the degree that I, on the basis of my Existenz, appropriate the symbols as my own.

In my consciousness of essential reality there takes place the decision as to whether I see in Being less than I am, or whether I sense in Being more than I am.

In the first instance I follow realism and materialism, positivism and idealism, which all agree in this one thing, that I see myself as something which, as the culmination of everything, has developed out of something earlier and lower, and which has grown out of something that was soulless, unfree, and, at first, indeed, even lifeless. This interpretation, however, founders on the fact that as it proceeds it provides no means for comprehending what man is capable of being, for comprehending his love, his thinking, or his knowing. This interpretation is ultimately reduced always to forms of naturalism, technicalism, or utilitarianism.

In the second instance, I surge up and beyond myself with the urge to yield to an "other," to reality itself. It is the movement of philosophizing which, bound to tradition and historical depth, finds its possible fulfillment in symbols. It is the Eros to which Being shows itself by simultaneously veiling and revealing itself in symbols. The interpretation of the symbols is the presence of the Being of reality.

C. *Slipping of the symbols.* In the belief in symbols there remains beyond all reflection an unreflectedness. Essential reality reveals itself only to our naïveté. This is restored again and again as long as we are still experiencing essential reality, even in the sublimest speculations of philosophy. The oneness of essential reality and intellectual certainty, of immediacy and reflection, of conditioned being and free responsibility, of force and suspension is lost in manifold ways. The slipping of the symbols is what is generally visible.

1. *Slipping into empirical reality (superstition):* If in the symbol the corporeal or the tangible becomes the thing itself, then the symbol is lost in favor of the phenomenon in the world. An object has turned into a handle, a support in the world by the worldly. In the empirically real, essential reality has vanished.

2. *Slipping into non-reality (allegory):* Reality is dissolved in mere interpreting. From signs and images, which are no longer anything but signs and images, the real is deduced. They are only mental allusions to it, not the objectivity of an original fundamental experience of the real.

3. *Slipping into detachment (aesthetic attitude):* Objectivization in poetry and art, as long as they are seriously pursued, is a means of preparation for, of making possible, of recalling, or of the play of anticipation of the experience of Existenz. Involvement in this experience is shown in the choice, in the seriousness of the awakened and confirmed demands, in the character of the

performance. But the wealth of this objectivization misleads one into making it the object of detached aesthetic contemplation. It becomes the impetus for the enjoyment of random emotions, or of unlimited possibilities. The play is confused with essential reality. The attenuation in detachment permits the content of the symbols to dissolve.

4. *Slipping into conceptualization* (*dogmatic metaphysics*): The thought contents of philosophy tend to make comprehensible that in the symbol which is essentially real. They lose their source when they have abandoned this reality in favor of rationally accessible knowledge. This again has many forms. In particular, Being is thought of as something cognizably real, as though it were an object of research, like things in the world. Then a construction of thoughts is regarded as the outline of this Being and is justified and proven without, however, the possibility of attaining in this way anything except cyphers. This dogmatic metaphysics is the descent from cypher-reading to presumed knowledge, by means of the intellect, of a Being which is inaccessible to the intellect. Furthermore, that which speaks in the cyphers is thought of as an obligation; so-called values and demands remain, a wealth of not only nonexisting, but of unreal values.

Since the cypher which becomes conscious also contains a moment of thinking and since thought itself can also become a cypher, the possibility of slipping is always there. The turn-about from the pure world of the cypher into rationality and into empirical reality is, for that reason, more compelling than the true cyphers themselves.

The dialectical and paradoxical twistings of transcending, one moment illuminating, and again effective in the right context, become empty and tiring with mere repetition. What was at first like a revelation turns into trite phrases. The objectivizations of the symbols step before concrete reality, in place of this reality, and are falsely applied as argumentations for the interpretation of reality and of what is practical and true in the world (a form of thinking which was almost predominant in the Middle Ages).

5. *Slipping to what is intentionally wanted (magic):* In cypher-reading surrender is achieved. To will to achieve it, or to pursue certain ends with them as a means destroys them. The source cannot be forced; to want to produce it makes it fail. Artificial symbols are not symbols, but traps. If one operates with symbols in order to aim at effects in the world, delusions occur; there is no real magic. Cyphers are not at one's command, are not means to an end, and cannot be produced, but they are accepted, found, and unconsciously experienced. I cannot control them but can only be conquered by them.

D. *Classification of the symbols.* If we ask about the *extent* of the realm of the cyphers then the answer is: everything objective can be a cypher. Cyphers are not new objects, but are newly consummated objects. Whatever of Being occurs in the world, becomes the material of the symbols.

A realm of symbols comes about through the circumstance that particular objects become historically the bearers of symbol-contents. Through paying attention to their function as symbols it is possible to organize the concretized objectivity of the cyphers in their mere objectness with an accompanying loss in their content. Typologies of symbols are outlined. These classifications are possible according to several *points of view,* for example, according to forms and contents.

Firstly, cyphers can be arranged according to the *form* of the relation in interpretation. If the symbol and what is symbolized are thought of as split, then the question is raised as to the manner in which one is in the other.

In the world there prevails a universal image- and metaphor-status of things for one another. Our language is a world of metaphors. In the cypher-status, however, that which signifies the cypher is, in fact, not to be separated from it. If I speak of the cypher as an interpreting, then this interpreting is itself a metaphor; being-a-metaphor is a metaphor for the original phenomenon of the revelation of Being in the cypher.

Thus the all-embracing metaphor is: through the cypher I participate in Being; being in the form of cypher is itself participation in Being. Through the cypher a *participation* in Being takes place at varying degrees of proximity or distance. All being is bound up with Being in a graduated linking. Every level, even the lowest, is still a cypher, participates in Being, is acknowledged, and has a glimmer of beauty: *omne ens est bonum.* If I dwell in it, everything becomes a cypher, illuminated by the ray of light out of the ground of Being, and every content becomes pale when this ray is extinguished. Then only the slag of matter-of-factness, of conceptuability, and of endless and indifferent determinations remains.

Being in the form of cypher reveals itself to love (as also in the beauty of mathematical thought-structures, of the mathematically constructed cosmos, and of living forms).

In participation, the mode of the relationship may be expressed in manifold additional metaphors. The metaphor is modified: the cypher contains in itself *being-as-a-sign* (the sign, and what is encountered in the sign, are essentially different, without similarity, without comparability, a mere referral) and *perceptible* [*anschaulich*] *being-as-a-symbol* (this perception bears a relationship to content). For thought, an *analogy* exists between the objective content and the actual Being (for example, between the empirical reality of the world and the essential reality of Transcendence, between the infinitude in the world and the infinity of the essentially real, or between all finite being and Being in itself: *analogia entis*). In the cypher lies a transcendental *model* (pattern, primal image) to which what is perceptible or conceptual corresponds more or less.

Secondly, cyphers can be classified according to the *contents* of the interpreting:

(a) The mass of historically available symbols lies between the poles of *universal,* everywhere recurring types, and of historical forms. The former may be classified as the typical basic symbols; the latter have to be elucidated as single steps in the process of the manifestation of Being. The universal gives a foundation and structure; the historically particular is what actually takes hold. The universal shows the abstract images, the historical, so to speak, the embodied form.

(b) Cyphers are either given in empirical realities or

are created as fabrications of man. What is given is the symbolism of all empirical being, the cypher-script of things themselves. What is created are the conceptions, ideals, and works—the cyphers of man with which the original cyphers are interpreted. The given would lead to the typology of all empirical being as a potential for cypher-status; what is created would lead to the typology of explicit symbols.

(c) Cyphers are created in the *perceptible imagery of myths* and in *conceptual speculations*. The former narrate and communicate in images; the latter move in the sequence of thought-consummation.

(d) Cyphers are *abstract* in their general structure and acquire *living form* in personal encounter—the former, for example, as the eternal feminine or as the Divine Mother, the latter in the particular historical mother and wife for this particular man; the former, the general spirit of Christ, the latter, Francis of Assisi for his disciples.

(e) Cyphers are empirical realities thrown into relief which make it evident within the whole that this is how it is; or they are *world images* in which the whole is apprehended; or they are *ideals* which hover, as it were, over empirical realities (like the *civitas dei* over the *civitas terrena,* or like the ideal of the saint, the hero, or the wise man over the ordinary man); or they are the *structures of Being* brought into relief in consciousness through the categories. Whenever the symbol-character becomes manifest, a circle is closed: out of mere presentness speaks the hidden essence; the hidden essence makes the presentness comprehensible.

An example of this is the Trinity. God becomes the Trinity with metaphors drawn from the world of experience, but the Trinity is also thought of as the basis of these phenomena in the world. The metaphor of the Trinity of God is the dialectical three steps which are to be found in all Being, especially in our inner life and intellectual development. These phenomena are, however, rather to be interpreted in reverse as the mirror and the likeness of the Trinity so that Augustine's *de trinitate dei* is perhaps just as much a knowledge of God as a knowledge of the soul. But this circle does not dissolve this whole as a delusion but is itself the cypher of Being which is just as lost in an objectivization into a presumed knowledge of God as in a reduction into empirically experienced triplicities. Other circles also arise between empirical reality and the language of Being, between the world image and knowledge, between the ideal and the reality of being-man.

4

The Ascent to the Reading of the Cypher-Script

Philosophizing is an initiation into the consciousness of Being. This initiation is accomplished first in the totality of philosophizing, not through a single thought. It takes place through the inner action which is accomplished by thinking, not by thinking as such.

The initiation achieves its fulfillment in the symbols which have become effective. To hear their language requires more than the methods of thinking. The impressiveness, depth, and force of the symbols is made manifest to that inner action achieved in the totality. In them philosophizing achieves the clarity and breadth from which it started as from a barely conscious seed. This hearing of the symbols is the first precedent and incomprehensible experience out of which philosophical thinking arises and towards which it strives.

This initiation takes place in leaps of clarification. That which becomes clear to me seems then to be that which I have actually always known. I remember the eternal in the form of an apparently new insight. The fulfillment of philosophy can at moments seem to participate in the knowledge of the creation.

We can speak of stages of initiation in philosophizing. The highest stage would be the penetration of objectivity in such a way that everything is a metaphor (cypher), nothing is without language, nothing is left to mere existence as the remains, as it were, of a non-being abandoned by God.

A. *The ascent to gliding*[8] *awareness.* The pure cypher speaks for a consciousness of Being for which everything objective and subjective is relative as a phenomenon in the movement, and sensual tangibility is overcome as the last stage of Being. This state of the consciousness of Being, in being one with all stages and modes of objectivity and subjectivity, would at the same time be gliding with respect to each one of its definite forms. I am aware of Being by not having become bound or grounded anywhere.

In this state the knowledge of reflection is unrestricted. I know that every stage or mode of Being, that the sensual present, and that deception and appearance are requisites for life; but I am able to recognize them as such, as that which they are. Knowledge does not overcome life but it has transformed it. Herein lies the decisive factor: whether I am able to achieve unconditional realization in time, knowing that all tangibility is a cypher; and whether, in such penetration of reality which attains a gliding state, I yet accomplish this with

---

8. Jaspers uses the word *"schweben"* both for the characteristic of thought which touches all forms of Being as it glides from one to another without adhering absolutely to any of them and also for that which, therefore, hovers suspended within and beyond the forms themselves.

the same force as one who is inwardly shackled to it [tangibility]. If I am not able to do this, then I lose both empirical reality and cypher, for if I permit the transcending to turn into impotent scepticism, then the tangible with its becoming-a-cypher transforms itself for me in aesthetic observation into an ineffective symbol. Through such a slipping of philosophizing I no longer arrive at a genuine foundering[9] but only at the loss or disappearance of life. I have lost the right to philosophize.

The building up of the philosophical awareness of Being is achieved in a sequence of stages, each of which, with its relativity, is at the same time preserved in the gliding. It is, to be sure, dissolved and transformed in reflection but not destroyed. In doing this, reflection can, however, also derange instead of preserving. It can lead to desperation in the loss of the consciousness of Being so that, instead of ascent, a precipitate descent takes place. Consciousness became the nemesis of simple immediacy.

This building up of the awareness of Being may be clarified by a comparison. I can observe my physical functions, such as the action of the heart or of respiration, can recognize them, can consciously follow them as my own, can understand them in their animal-physiological function, and can, as it were, adopt them as my own. The knowledge of physiological corporeality leaves their function untouched. Life on the higher stage knows about that which comes earlier without being able to disturb it, indeed, rather enhances and secures it by holding it within standards appropriate to it.

But this is not the only possibility. Observation can

---

9. Cf. Introduction.

be disturbing. Knowledge leads to painful apperception of what happens to alterations of the function, for instance, to hypochondriac developments in fear and anxiety, to tormenting emotions and ailments. Yet the function always remains a necessary requisite for life and must remain so. If it should fail, then every higher function of life which depends on it would disappear with it.

It is a fundamental feature of human physical life, in contrast to that of the animal, that man knows more or less about his body and influences it. He can become the physician of his body or its destroyer, whereas the animal, who must surrender completely to the biological course, must live for his body without being able to see beyond it or into it. The influence of man on his body occurs in manifold ways in a manifold sense. One way is that of the conscious appropriation and exercise of physical life in the service of the soul. With my knowledge I will take my body in hand, will improve its functions, put them in the service of higher goals, from the relaxation exercises of modern psycho-therapy to the mystical breathing techniques which are a special feature of Asiatic philosophical practice.

The question is, how far can a body be ruined by unreasonable knowledge on the part of the soul; and secondly, how far is the management of physical life able to enhance the soul; and finally, how far can even a failing body be yet sustained by a reasonable soul.

This comparison of the attitude of reflection towards all stages of the consciousness of Being, up to gliding awareness, with the attitude of knowledge towards life, shows, in both, the twofold possibility in the course of the process of awareness: either knowledge and disturbance, or knowledge and, with it, a raising of the lower states from the position of the higher ones. The knowledge which can disturb can also enhance and can protect against disturbances and remove disturbances which have occurred. Furthermore, it is common to both that the earlier stages must be preserved and elevated in the process of penetration in order to carry and make possible the later ones. Only when we remain with clarity in all stages of the knowledge of objectivity and unfold them, can we attain the meaning of the higher stages which would sink into nothingness without the others.

In philosophizing, the stages in the gliding of the knowledge of Being lead up to the point where the resting-place of Being sets a goal for the gliding. Every mode of the knowledge of Being is, as it were, a standpoint which is surpassed. In philosophizing we achieve and practice these modes of surpassing. Finally, however, genuine consciousness of Being is not a point of view. For there is no longer a standpoint outside of it or above if from which the consciousness of Being could be viewed. On the contrary, here is that point from which all other standpoints are seen as standpoints or as stages for getting here.

For this gliding there are two presuppositions: all objectivity is to be grasped in its relativity—and the support in the distant One must not be lost.

B. *The ascent through the grasping of all objectivity.* Because all the stages of objectivity are presupposed in order to swing up to the last one, and because, further-more, the breadth of the realization of each step is requisite for the depth of the last, therefore, he who philosophizes has at every step an irrevocable will to the object. Every mode of being-an-object must con-stantly surround him, as air and nourishment surround the body. Not to omit any mode, to be present again and again in every mode, and to seize methodically in every presence what is essentially real, is a fundamental trait of philosophizing itself.

Philosophizing began with astonishment. Astonishment turns into questioning.

An answer is given by research, by illumination, by reflection, or by affirmation. Each time a world of objectivity arises.

(a) *Research*: In the sciences the methods of ex-periencing the empirically real are developed, and definite knowledge of objects is found. The sciences help me in training my ability to see and to observe. With scientific organs I go through the world. I try to be present in all activities, in sociological functions, in intercourse with people, in technical skills, and I try to raise whatever I experience into consciousness, to transform it into knowledge, and to experience it as something new and better.

(b) *Illumination*: What we are and can be as Ex-istenz and what is present to us as a mode of the En-compassing, is illuminated by thoughts which, since the beginning of philosophizing, are not actually knowledge but are that which addresses itself to us in the form of wisdom and maxims, thoughts which do not put a world of objectivity at our disposal but which call to us [as potentialities]. As the illumination of Existenz and the philosophy of the Encompassing this way comes into full consciousness.

(c) *Reflection*: I seek fundamental knowledge in the totality of the sciences, in the illuminations and affirmations, and in the categories and methods of which thinking in all these directions makes use. Thereby, in the breadth of its forms, in the origins, in the all-sidedness of its possibilities as at present achieved, my fundamental knowledge becomes clear. This I achieve in philosophical logic as the order of my knowing consciousness.

(d) *Affirmation*: Authentic being becomes realized in the cypher. All the modes of objectivity, every form of thinking, of research, of illumination, of reflection are in the service of the deepening of the perceptible cypher-script.

Research may, indeed, at first destroy the cypher-script of the myths insofar as its corporeality contained a moment of untruth and superstition. It is, however, the intention of research to lead the way towards a true cypher-script. Cypher-script without research is deceiving. Universal research must lead to the boundary where the highest astonishment and the most penetrating cypher-script become possible.

The cypher-script of Being must be read with the help of the cypher-script brought forth by men. What myth and revelation have said I want to understand and know about even though it be in a philosophical transformation. Whatever part of it has become objective in poetry, art, and religion, becomes the organon of philosophizing. In philosophizing itself the will to objectivity forces itself into the clarity of the cypher-script of thought which has become objective.

C. *The ascent to a Divinity.* The decisive factor for all consciousness, for inner action, for the ethos, for freedom, for existence and reason, is whether and how the reality of God is the measure of all things.

But the one God is distant; the completely "other" is entirely hidden. It is, therefore, not only easy but almost compelling for reason and sensual experience to deny Him. He cannot be deduced from any single phenomenon, cannot be perceived as Himself in anything specific. If everything is related to Him and everything comes from Him, it is not in any comprehensible way.

His distance makes the ascent to Him almost always falter again and again. We flutter our wings of philosophizing and rise above the ground only for a few moments and only slightly. In another metaphor, we remain stranded on the way to Him, or by plunging in vain directly into the reality of God, we miss the way.

(a) *We are stranded on the way*: We learn by observation of the "souls" of the elements, of Nature, of the living, of the landscape, of the cosmos; we experience the "forces"; we obey manifold demands of the good, beautiful, true, practical, and vital. From time to time we believe that we are face to face with an ultimate, must serve it and ought not deny it. This ultimate cannot be reduced to a denominator. There are the many gods which are in competition and in conflict with one another. There are the demons which rule the world. In

countless variations of historical form we remain stranded
in a mode of demonology and have lost sight of the one
God because there is no experience of Him either external or internal. He is that from which experience first
obtains meaning and guidance, in the face of which the
false ultimate becomes foreground, question, movement,
and task. In philosophical thought this fixation takes
place when we think of all-inclusive reality in absolutized
categories as a basic law of Being, as necessity, as growth,
as the will to power, as an order of monads, etc. These
latter ideas, like the former demonological view, have
their value and their truth as a language en route; they
become false when they are assumed to grasp reality
in its totality as the content of faith. Theories of a meta-
physical character, by analogy with theories of natural
science or with world images, are a monstrous delusion
if, instead of cyphers along the way in gliding and
foundering they permit the one God to be forgotten.
Then they force man into a corner, rob him of his freedom and of his nobility.

(b) *We miss the way by wanting to rush directly
into the reality of God*: The fascination of the thought
of the One fatally devaluates the world, the fullness of
its phenomena and our own life. However, we manage
to get to the One only through the world, only with its
phenomena and the historicity of our life. If we grasp
it directly it becomes empty. Abstract monotheism becomes a negative concept and a negating action in the
attitude towards faith. Everything is nothing. However,
this insight, fundamentally true, permits the one God
Himself to become nothing if, instead of pushing ahead

restlessly along the way, it considers itself already to be the fulfillment.

Our possible fulfillment lies in *mediation*. The ascent to the one God passes through the world of phenomena. The transformation of the world into a mediation between us and the one God is its transformation into *being-a-cypher*. That essential reality is itself the one God we learn only indirectly in the empirical realities of the world through the language of the world. We learn it through our ascent in awareness of the cyphers, each of which permits us no rest and propels us into further flight. If there were a direct experience of the one God, it would be incommunicable and could, in the course of time, verify, recall and confirm itself again only indirectly through phenomena in the world. There is only one road to the one God along which everything that is, everything we encounter, everything we ourselves are and do becomes transparent. This becoming transparent is the becoming-a-cypher, and this becoming-a-cypher moves into the boundless depths of developing meanings, not one of which conclusively fulfills a meaning knowably. We should always hold ourselves open for the cypher-script whose communication we cannot force by intention and plan. Everything which is, must become a cypher. It is the earnestness which operates in us out of that which can appear by the standards of everyday reality as dream and play.

Striving beyond all mediations along the road, we would like *to form an image of God Himself*. What we attain in this way is again always only cyphers of the Divinity. Yet God is not a cypher but reality itself. The imaging of God is called theology. Theology never gets any further than an intellectual conception of the language of cyphers. It has truth under the condition that it preserves the tension toward the absolutely distant, the very "other" of Transcendence. Every imaging of God which believes it can grasp Him Himself other than in the vanishing mediation of cyphers falls short of the mark. We can only penetrate into phenomena and seek to discover the ground of the mystery. If we do so, we speak in cyphers.

If I renounce every perceptible cypher, then, in formal transcending, I open the space for speculation which breaks through the world towards Transcendence. If I try to bring the Divinity nearer to myself with cyphers, then such cyphers fail without exception. Whether I think of God as the One and its emanations; as the seed, the source, the ground of the development of all things; as the overseer or the architect of the world; as the One and its creation out of nothingness; as personality; as the Trinity—it is always the same thing: everything is at best metaphor and pointer. If I should possess all possible metaphors; if I were to think of everything in God and not omit anything—His love and His anger, His righteousness and His mercy; if I refer to Him everything which occurs in the world; if, in addition, I add in my thinking everything which might be, I will never, in this infinite play of cyphers, reach God himself.

It would be different if there were a direct and exclusive *revelation* of God. Such a revelation has been claimed. This claim is the foundation of the Indian and

Judeo-Christian-Islamic religions. But such a claim of revelation is a usurping by individual people and groups of people of the truth for their special historicity as having common validity for all men. It cannot be denied that in such a form Transcendence has spoken historically for men everywhere. But men confused cyphers with Being itself. Even externally the majority of mutually conflicting revelations speaks against all of them. It is the arrogance of men, which is disguised in submission to such revelation, to demand of all other men, under the name of humility, submission to their own truth and to themselves as its representative.

The contents of claimed revelation, when stripped of their absolutisms and their character of exclusiveness, are to be adopted philosophically in the form of cyphers. An example is the Christ myth. Jesus is, to be sure, not God in the world. No man is God. The distance between man and God is infinite. The paradoxical interpretations, which point to the reality of the God-man, cannot delude the person, who, conscious of his humanness, preserves the distance for himself and all other men. But the Christ myth is a cypher for the justification of the cypher as mediation between God and man. By the belief in Christ we are wrongly faced with the alternative of choosing between either a deification of the world in the pinnacle of the God-man or a lost, soulless, God-forsaken world which is opposed to the infinitely distant God-Creator as the completely "other." That the distant God speaks in the cyphers of the world and of man and accomplishes His mediation, indicates a never-ending conceiving and realizing of man in the world and not that

God has to become man in the flesh. Rightly, however, there is in the Christ myth the indication that everything human has in it the possibility of relatedness to God, God-nearness, and that the way to God goes through the world and through the reality of our historically to be determined human nature, and not by-passing the world. Philosophy must guard man against usurpation while recognizing at the same time a cypher truth in the claims of the usurper.

On the other hand, the ascent to the one God is to be protected against an *attitude without faith* which can be clothed in misleading thoughts. The actuality of the one God is undermined, for example, by the following consideration. The one God is an idea which brings us, like a magic potion, as it were, to our freedom. The idea does, indeed, make the highest demands upon us and opens up the widest space for us. With this idea man swings himself up out of the constraints of his existence and the narrowness of his impulses. When it has been said that the idea of God is necessary for the control of despotism, malice, and the ill-will of the average man, for the peace of society and for the reliability of intercourse and harmony, it might now be added that the idea of God is necessary so that man may come to himself, so that man may become free of all the world for himself. Even in this sense one might repeat Voltaire's statement that if there were no God, He would have to be invented.

Such thoughts are, however, as senseless as they are destructive. An invented God cannot have such an effect (even if he might perhaps through deception of the masses temporarily bring them into submission through fear of punishments in Hell). Only an actual God is capable of this. The man who invents God and does not believe in Him does not experience the uplift. The man who, while deluding himself, believes in Him, would bring about what, according to his nature, would never be comprehensible from delusion. In such a merely seeming-to-understand, that which is Existenz and Transcendence is, in the categories of vital and psychological causality, robbed of its meaning and its essential reality.

The one God cannot be acquired in a definite manner in an exclusive way. Only in the totality, out of historical depth, in the Encompassing of everything thinkable and everything that can be experienced, is the ascent possible to the One who is not less, not emptier, not more abstract than the world, but who encompasses the world in which everything, through the fact that it is in relation to Him, can be elevated to its highest potentialities.

There are no directions as to how the ascent may be accomplished. Here it is as in all essentially philosophical procedure: what is decisive each time happens only once and cannot be generally anticipated. It would be a mistake to presume that with the pointing to the foundation and mode of philosophical movement a fulfillment is already given, a program set up, or perhaps even the consciousness of Being mediated in its content. It would be a false expectation that in such indications a knowledge is acquired by which one could be guided.

Illumination by philosophizing is not a guide for behavior. Loosening of the possibilities of origin is not mediation of substance.

The origin lies in God. To each man must be given from Him what he becomes through the fact that he begins to perceive Being and how he begins to perceive it. The communication of philosophy does not give essential reality but makes it possible to become aware of it.

Philosophy awakens, makes one attentive, shows ways, leads the way for a while, makes ready, makes one ripe for the experience of the utmost.